Standing by Thistles

Anne MacLeod

To Isobel + Bob
with love

Anne

SCOTTISH CONTEMPORARY POETS SERIES

SCOTTISH CULTURAL PRESS

First published 1997
Scottish Cultural Press
Unit 14, Leith Walk Business Centre
130 Leith Walk
Edinburgh EH6 5DT
Tel: 0131 555 5950 • Fax: 0131 555 5018

British Library Cataloguing in Publication Data
A catalogue record for this book is available from the British Library

ISBN: 1 898218 66 8

The publisher acknowledges subsidy from the Scottish Arts Council
towards the publication of this book

Printed and bound by
BPC-AUP Aberdeen Ltd

Scottish Contemporary Poets Series
(for further details of this series please contact the publishers)

Contents

Anne MacLeod was born in 1951 of Anglo-Irish parents, the second of five children. She has lived most of her life in or near Inverness, studying medicine in Aberdeen. After gaining her degree she returned to Inverness and has worked there ever since, latterly as a dermatologist serving communities throughout the Highlands. She is married, with four children.

Standing by Thistles is her first collection of poems but her poems and short stories have been widely published. She is interested in longer fiction, children's and adult, and is currently immersed in her first adult novel.

She counts herself lucky to have come from a family which had strong links with the Irish oral tradition; a home where song and story were always important.

for Gregor and the young Sinatra

Acknowledgements

The author and publisher wish to thank the editors of the following publications in which some of these poems have appeared: *Aberdeen University Review, Asheville Poetry Review, Cencrastus, Chapman, Kuna Pipi, Lines Review, Northwords, Original Prints 4, Second Shift, West Highland Free Press, Wordworks (Highland Printmakers), X124.*

The author also wishes to thank her family, Jim, Joanne, Alasdair, Catriona and Alex for their support and patience.

you say I am not passionate

There will be no end

There will be no end to the joy, my love.
We will stand together as the stars
sweep the Cuillin, rounding into morning
the bright new morning of the tender heart.
And where we sing, the song will be a fine one
and where we dance, our steps will never fail
to tap the spring of life, of love and laughter
timeless as stars, the wheeling, circling stars
that dance and sing, and sing and dance again:
and there will be no end
to the joy

Eve

Slip inside my skin. I'm
shiny and thin
Sinuous
A natural snake
I'll bed you and
shed you
and shred you and
slither –
you'll shiver, I'll hug
when we slide
on the rug
Shag me
the natural snake
My scales slip so sweetly
my tongue forks so
neatly. I
swallow
       completely

Pieta

A broken body
heavy on my withered breast;
it is not my son

in Lebanon and
Ireland, in El Salvador;
it is not my son

in China where they
charged me for the bullet;
it is not my son

they brought him to my
silence. 'Take your son,' they said;
it is not my son

a broken body
heavy on my withered breast;
it is not my son

what is not seen

your canvas tells its own story
draws us imperceptibly
towards the sea you celebrate
in pale uneasy strokes
a sea unquiet, empty as the room is
as the chair
as the face that looms in shadow
as a mother
as a mother
your canvas screens the bright still life
stretched behind that sea
vibrant, incomplete
promising

Our lichened pear tree

> bears uneven fruit. One year
we plucked the straightest of the crop, bitter still

and sprayed the woody skin; bright gold on dark fir-green
the silver tinsel strands and scarlet blaze

ribboned our dying Christmas fires.
We left on the tree the smallest, poorest pears

wizened and bent, to satisfy the birds
shimmering in the frost, appease what ancient god

saps winter's hoar, breathes life in lichened twig
swells buds in spring.

After the plum's brief flower, the pear tree sang
lacing the earth and sky and silvered bough

with beauty pure and clear, with greater love
than this veiled tree could bear. Thus, unfulfilled,

spring's bloom breeds summer's fall, unripening fruit.
Some trees we cut and burn. The pear tree stands

purely to smile in spring, charge new-green grass
with bleak confetti showers; we bow mute as the petals'
         withering.

So much that flowers will fail, each death
a littered harmony, melding sweet destructiveness

lasting dissolution the subtext as we rot. Our theme
is not impenetrable: we seed and bud and swell

die, swell again, diminishing. Ripe flesh, decaying,
salts the universe, engenders seed; only the bones remain

like wizened pears in winter, prophets lost, scattering
good brown earth. This tree will never touch the sky

nor will its fruit grow tender, however tended; this tree
hoards its lichen and what pears it may. It bows

before the storm, ageing, until spring, weathering
ancient dreams, bears them away.

For Mattie

In Ireland you are young
your heart sings
your eyes dance brighter than the star-shocked skies
what do you not dream?
All the world is yours;
but Maggie dies.

Far in the sullen north
you end your days
alone and lame, husband and son both lost:
your heart-song, undiminished
haunts you still.
You sing, star-crossed.

Song of sixpence

Each Sunday she made apple pie
with neat fingers
plied the pastry quilt around
the fruit
      no serpent here, no tree,
apples cored and peeled, sliced, tossed
in caster sugar into the once-white enamel
tin, its blue edge wandering

she worked at speed
to sheath the frosted flesh before
the rot could
set pastry leaves feathering
the blackbird's open
beak
the beaten glaze
and neat fork-pricking

unhardened
she risked all in the snaking fire
each Sunday, with burnt fingers

Stir-fry
(for Liz, in memory)

I cheated, of course, with the sauce.
A jar provided sweet and sour, with extra pineapple
(don't forget the pineapple)
though I hate cooking, I sliced pork fillet
in succulent strips, which I fried in olive oil
with garlic, onion, carrot, apple; all I could find
at such an hour, after an evening of poetry
your gift to me and my small family.

We stayed late at the reading, as you had expected.
You waited for the stir-fry, expectant.
I chopped and tossed, fretted over sticky rice
cheating with the sauce. No-one seemed to mind;
we talked into the night, chopsticks discarded
for spoon and fork, your honesty uncompromising.

There is a poem Iain did not read that night
of a Chinese restaurant, and wonderful menu
strangely understood; this lack of distance
Aonghas would have flown, scart's wing
grazing lonely kyles. Yet here was
no contention, no lack of warmth or grace:
such lightness as yours did not need extra pineapple
even when the chopsticks danced in your hands.
Did I show you those poems? I wish

I could read them to you now, tonight, when the distance
is no longer tangible, the menu uncertain; loss
inescapable.
And were you here tonight
I would not cheat with the sauce.

home

still, when I round the
corner, your window shining
with no light in it

Mirrors

A white house, filled with full length mirrors,
very hard to clean, must tell you something.
I mean
the owner must be houseproud,
sex-mad, have no children,
no dogs either. Plain
vain.
I didn't buy it, though I did frequent it.
I rented.

Human nature

The men who come to my door
all have wives; my friends.
These men call late
on slender pretexts, with no
prior warning.
Often I do not let them in.
I've lost my faith
in human nature.

Cafe society

I am not yet
so set in my ways
but when I am older
wiser and richer
and live in the south of France
cafe society will be somewhat
finer than the Tea Cosy

Kiosk

Perhaps you think I don't feel
the cold. I do.
I'm lonely too, my corner
vulnerable. Exposed.
The tales I could tell!
But I don't. Of course I don't.
Who would trust me
if I did? Who would come
if all they said was
broadcast through the neighbourhood?

Don't you wonder, don't you glance
as you pass me?
Don't you stare?
I've seen it often
artless appraisal masking
bare impertinence.
You glare into my depths,
note who's with me,
but it's not enough.
You want the substance too.

I share it all, and never criticise.
I welcome all.
I never shut my door.
Sometimes it's your money handed over,
your breath, your lips, your hand
on my receiver.

Great grandad and the actress

My great grandfather ran off with an actress
not Lily Langtree, but someone just as famous:
wearing three suits and the family savings
he strutted abroad till the money ran out.
Then the bold lady left great grandad bereft
and, somewhat abashed, he returned to his wife
who took him
            the patient, who took him
                      the saint
who took him, the fool, and made no complaint

that's what they told me.
Could it be true?
What would do if great grandad left you?

Roses

Childhood. A feast of roses.
Waste ground behind our house
where bramble, gorse and briar grew
sharp thorns of adversity,
flowered too.
I plucked dog-roses, banquets of them,
tried to plant the bleeding stems.
They died.
They always did,
tears and blood and withered petals.

'It's bouquets, not banquets,'
smug older sister.
Wrong, wrong, wrong.
It should be banquets.

Persephone's daughter

My mother never gave me pomegranates,
did not buy them, would not have them in the house
and little wonder. Were not they

the source of her undoing
deep in the underground?
Had she not tasted seven pomegranate seeds

she would have escaped, emerging fresh
from Picadilly, sweet as violets
to Eros' tender flight.

My mother never brought me pomegranates
and I endured the lack impatiently:
misunderstanding what she did not say

till I too tasted darkly and the fruit
tinctured my flesh;
no longer free, I roam

half the year dead, endure
my black love's lust
desiring more

Redbreast

I am with you in the dark days, the cheerless time
when night stumbles early and dawn strives late
to lighten winter's cold malevolence.
Ice will not fill your belly.

In frozen grief I sing, my bleeding breast
a haemorrhage of love, of warmth, of light
spilled unawares upon a thorn-sharp world
ice cannot satisfy;

and still the notes float in the north wind's blast
echoing earth's true fire I sought and won
out of the deepest chasm, earth's true heart –
where is the ice that can deny the spring?

Within my breast the blood and fire burn
and I will be consumed in my turn.

Kindling

You rise to mend the fire
challenging the hearth
taut in concentration and fine white linen
as you coax the flames, oblivious
to other, older fires
crackling in the kindled air

conversation with magic stones

only later did I think about the stones
they danced between us, neolithic runes,
bronze images, brazen as the high, red sun
that shocked;
                    our weathered tune
rose to a sky as blue
as understanding

in bed with a poet

your resonance enthralled
I did not expect such pleasure
voice and words flowed over me
charmed smooth sheets
swung lightly in the curtains
on my high sweet bed

I should maybe
buy the book

Cassiopeia

Together we outdid the stars, my
daughter and I, and she in any company
shone brighter than the moon, cancelled
constellations of doubt.

Perhaps I should have kept this to myself.
Perhaps I should have hidden such
shining youth, doused it in a
black shawl, vanquished it. I
raised my daughter knowing
she would leave.

american mystery 1

I don't know why the lone ranger
flaunted his spurs
to william tell's overture
and silver bullets
was there any point?
the great unwashed in wildest west
were not the great undead
except the extras
who conceivably
might have played
in dracula
but not before
the matinee

the black mask
a dead giveaway
hiyo silver
haway to transylvania
gessler guzzling
the big apple

a useful substance, salt

a useful substance, salt
in the hand
in the broth
too many cooks
over your shoulder

in the wound

psyche 4

they fed me dreams of love
nights lost on satin cushions
a kind and tender prince
to soothe my cares, satisfy
they fed me dreams of love
I grew fat

he came at night in book
and video, page and screen;
my senses thrilled with each new penetration
each clear reverberation
fed my dreams
I grew fat

I did not like the fat
a slave to appetite
I slept in his dark
restless, satiated
then looked upon the prince and fled

Aphrodiet beckoned
Fly me
Work your butt off, she said
Slob. I said
I'd try it

so now I soar in thin light
dream of cake

psyche 5

late in the smothered dark, you called me beautiful
yet would not wait for day's redeeming light
on silken skin, warily sought, freely given

I did not ask your name that first time
night succeeded restless night, my body
less my own, defined by love, star-ridden

but morning found me empty; breasts, bruised moons
oceans ebbing from my parted thighs
and deep inside, a longing to own what had possessed me

you ran, left me in passion's house
my country still
though no-one holds me fit for loving
lust
        my bleak domain

the long day I endure, but night is hard
stars burn

Walberswick

In Walberswick the lilies danced
slow delicate life and you
delicately painted them
elegant, erect.
Fritillary – snakeshead lilies –
flowers you might well
have fashioned in a moment's
art-nouveau experiment.
Life was not sweet, and yet the calm
elegance remains
order imposed on chaos, anarchy resigned
to the smooth curve of nature's architectural entropy.
In Walberswick the lilies danced
as if for you alone
slow delicate death.

Icarus

The cloud sea drifts into the morning sky.
Under your wing I linger, would remain
safe in the aqua fading into blue.
Soft clouds below obscure the sodden earth
the mountains' dark insistence, and the sprawl
of cities forced into the light of day
out of the night's warm slumber.
                                        Here with you
curled in your arms, love-drowsed, I do not hear
the break of day, the passing of our dawn,
the morning's dappled call. I can ignore
the sun that plays upon your golden wings,
warm now and soft; too late I wake and turn
shocked by the sudden heat, the burning wax –
surely we will not fall?

spinning nettles

spinning nettles, you called them
no matter how often corrected, how
great the pain inflicted
by stinging fibres;
you'd search for dock leaves
cursing spinning nettles, while I imagined
hands martyred in vain
twining cruel hairs, the spindle primed

now I have learned
hair shirts are won from nettles
dried nettle stings
do not

Flax

A woman
weaves the sea,
linen thread.
                    White waves
translucent
shuttle at her
feet
        dip into greener
rock
        deepen the blue
horizon.
                    Sky
fade.

A woman weaves the
sea
        withered
stems.

Looking for Dolphins

i

I was looking for dolphins
not seals, though seals there were
skulking in the ebb-tide with
great black heads, like labradors
breasting the waves' uncertain carnage.
Here at the Point, the currents met,
strong, impassioned,
precipitating plankton, refuse; fish
fed here, and dolphins hunted.
Seals did too.
I looked for fins in vain.
The dolphins did not jump for me.

ii

You knew about seals
taught me how to trap the selkie.
Hide the skin, you said,
then they're fixed in human form,
condemned to an eternity
of breast-stroke.

I shrugged, removed your hand,
my skin apparently intact.

Tea-dance

Your arms have grown so thin, skin hangs
like wet rag on the wasted flesh.
Lifting you is hard,
not for the lack of weight.
'You'll need to take me through.
I couldn't use that thing.'
I push the commode back,
'Let's sit you up, then.'

Movement leaves you breathless.
'No, let me do the work…
see? I've got the chair.
I'll turn you round. Like dancing.'
'I never did like dancing,'
Your arms slide round my neck
but there is no strength in them,
'Never got the hang of it.'

'Let me do the work.'
I guide you to the swaying chair.
'Dad put rollers in.'
'Sit back there, Mum.'
'But will you take them out?'
your voice breaks now,
'I don't expect… can't expect…
your father
              to stay single.'

You do not look at me. I sigh,
'Of course I'll do your hair,'
ease the chair this last time
through the door
down the cluttered hall
and past the living room
where Dad makes tea you cannot drink,
an offering of love

Birdsong

Blue sky
enough to make a sailor's hat
wan, washed-out, drenched in evening birdsong:
you told the birds by note. I
never listened

After you'd gone

After you'd gone, I filled the grate
with flowers and greenery
stripped from the windblown garden
between sulking showers.
I could not fill the empty hours so easily,
would not ask your pardon.

I tried to recreate the dancing flame
yesterday's warmth, discarded
leaving us burnt and chilled;
it hurts, this stealth,
this parting unfulfilled,
fitful fire sparking sap and thorn.

Orion dancing

Leaving you
has always been the hardest.
Frost stabs the bitter night,
winter fire
sings in the north, while
on the farthest hill,
Orion dances.

Disciples of the dance

We are all disciples of the dance
You and I and the beautiful women before us
who stretch their limbs in harmony, linger in the chorus –
we are all the victims of romance

You and I, and the beautiful women of the chorus
are all victims of romance
They strain their limbs in unison, linger before us
everyone entitled to entrance

all the victims of romance
Stretching limbs in lingering harmony we chorus
spread our wings in agony, suffering the more as
innocent disciples of chance
We are all the victims of the dance

Choosing songs

We sing of lost love, happy in the art
of choosing songs as once we chose those loves
now lost. We sing in harmony, our part
to laugh and weep as music interweaves

sorrow and hope, themes that demand contrition.
Our songs confess, yet as the notes rebound
single yet double, love's brief absolution
fades, the sundered lyric slyly turns

stifles naked melody, requites
rhythm and rhyme; blank dissonance
incites new fear as love inexorable
falters and fails in minor cadences.

We cannot live in song, and yet we live
and love and leave, and live and love
                                    and love

You say I am not passionate

You say I am not passionate
not true
My heart does somersault
but not for you

Oran Mor

Oran Mor

There are songs, and there is oran mor
piobaireachd of the human chanter –
who will sing if these notes fail?
Who can bind the wind?

Reeds bend before the storm, flowers
fade upon the machair, seeds
driven by the bean sith fervour of the gale
into droning hibernation

at the island's edge. The sun will
rise again, but to what new music? The seed
may fall on lazy-beds of bitter generation,
or germinate

in bleak despair on the bare shingle,
one step from extinction.

Reading

You read your poems twice, once in
Gaelic, once in English.
Sometimes, in the Gaelic, you stumble over words,
repeating them to get the music right. As if
the language is not one you are used to. As if
the spell could be shattered by a misplaced vowel,
the culture fade with lost internal rhyme.

My neighbour stumbles too, when I ask him.
His speech is slow, precise, as he sounds the puirt-a-beul
of the tongue he has known since childhood.
Perhaps these days he must think in English, but
when he is asleep, will his dreams
be twice as long?

Shop windows

In shop windows in Stornoway
I saw
a black lace dress reduced
several books of poetry
earrings a bible rabbit slippers and
Concerto the definitive cage
for a canary

This island

would be beautiful, he
said, If there were trees. A row
of trees beside the road. That's
what we want. Beautiful.

Then, when you were driving, there'd
be something to look at.
But they'd
block the sky, I said.
He shook his head.

In Stornoway

it's raining. Grey summer tears
spatter the tourists,
children in the street
flush in winter uniform, blue
jeans, dark skirts. First day
back at school. Another
summer

overhead, a plane drones
wistful in the stratus, tossed
in drifting air, brief insect in a
wider world, above the island
wavering

sea drifts blue to green to
distant Coigach, flanks the
Summer Isles, Assynt's bones
scarred, exposed

dark skirts cover
what they cannot hide

a mhathair

open your window
look out on the morning
born, cold and white
the sea calm, unburdened
empty waves ebbing

dawn on the machair
no warmth in the bleak sun
no lamp in your window
curtains drawn close
against morning's unfolding

blue curtains, threaded
with ribbon and roses
screening the machair
no thorns on the roses
that tether your window

but new roses stab
the year's dawn, and the sea
deflowers the sand
where I lie
tide-worn

a mhathair
open your window

Another wedding

I sit on three-week grass, grown soft and long,
to view the photographs; another wedding
another clear blue sky, another world
and girls, big-boned and blonde, with Lewis eyes.
They did you proud in Canada. (The bride
forgot her veil. The dress looked fine – but think,
three bridesmaids and no veil!) That white dress swirls
from Sarnia to Callanish, the eyes
from Callanish to Sarnia, unveiling generations;
sisters, brides, spin gently in the clear
unyielding years.

Your white dress swirls around you, and below
the lingering island waves a calm farewell
in moonlight and the psalm that single ray
illumines;
this bride forgot her veil. Your camera
exalts her open beauty, while the eyes
from Callanish to Canada seal disparate generations.
There is one more distant, diffident; we see
you
        dancing
through the trees.

Aros

O dark boy
with your black eyes shining
why do you treat me
so reverently?
Do I
look so old?

You bring me food
and wine,
a communion, undoubtedly,
but keep your
brightest smiles
for the young girl opposite.

She will not love you
as I could.
She will not
write this poem

Port Righ harbour

eight o' clock
Port Righ harbour
passes for busy
one boat loading noisily
another
in the distance
slices through the bay
spills silver wake
across the morning
eight o'clock
sun above
hot on my skin
sun in ripples
dances through closed eyes
the sky too blue
for argument
sky sun
water sun
collude
shimmer in unison
like you and I
my love
like you and I

Cuckoo of Sligachan

I hear you, cuckoo, high above
my nest of wind and reed
From Roineval to Gillean, your
call resounds, insistent

You, the harbinger of Spring; you
the self-inflicted messenger
that fills the nest
excluding
ejecting what within
lay peaceful and in ignorance

Cuckoo,
I hear. I will not rise
to meet your early greeting
emotional, irrational as
children on the shore. I have
exorcised the spark of
immoderate ambition
My rock is black, irregular
I sink in crevices
as deep and sharp as gabbro
can procure

Cuckoo
I will not sing. My
unstable compromise
to rhythms that reach far beyond
the waves
of wind and sea
resides in complete consolidation
from cuillin peak to stream, from
pinnacle to scree
should I sing, the sky would fall
mountains desist

Do you know
what binds the land in grim
submission? Or is your song
unheeding after all
a mere reflex to changing light
rising temperature? Does your fluting
bring destruction on us all?

A single ray of light
may distort the universe
a butterfly unleash
the waterfall

Tomb of the eagles

They buried me with eagles
high on a wind-wracked cliff
in Isbister. (That's what I
hear you call it. We had
another name, a different tongue.)
A striking tomb, an eagle's
lair – a warning
the people of the dog could not
ignore.
      For what are dogs to eagles
that sweep and soar and plummet
all claws and fearsome beak,
wings wider than a house,
strong as the winter wind?

Dogs must hunt in packs,
bay and howl, tear the flesh.
We drop in silence
alone upon our prey

and you will not know the moment
but for us it is eternal
the life-long falling
till time stands still
claws flexed around, within
about

time stands

we had another name, a different
time
Now I have been taken
by the people of the dog
(no eagle would rake up
old bones and worry them
like this)
I sit upon a scrap of cloth
black, thin and shiny

I learn the habits
of the dog.

– This is Grandad, she barks
and hauls me from my place
– Your Grandad of two hundred
generations back; two hundred
times the genes have danced
between him and you
but he is you

Never. I am eagle to the core.
I am eagle to the claws
and beak.
There is no dog in me

She hands me round, an
offering; they
shudder, back away.
On these days, I grow strong,
feel the beak within my
skull.
          You sniff me?
You're a dog all right.
And what about the smell?
It's dog, all dog-
smoke, fire and panting.
Sniff me? Smell yourself

– He died at thirty-five, she whines
Quite old. We'll put him
back – carefully – oh.
I didn't mean to bump him

She does that every time.
If I could stand,
if I had arms and legs
and voice, I'd show her

even the women shuddered
at my roar, stopped
work in field or
fire, stopped chewing at the
leather, looked at one another

even the women

if I had wings and claws
and beak, I'd teach her

she would not know the moment
but for me, eternal
the life-long falling
till time stands still
claws flexed around, within
about

Burnt mound

Dig carefully:
the charred accumulations,
midden and stone, obscure
a hearth of slate,
stone-burned domesticity,
a fire smoored.
The graying embers wait
two thousand years – for what?
A bellow's kiss?

Prince Charming
be an archaeologist.

Turf

(Earl's Palace, Birsay)

To tell the truth, a spade
is not as good, cuts edges
too bluntly, you can't get

the angle. You do the job
right with a knife.
Turf withers quickly

this time of year. The beasts
need the water, and who'd
take it from them?

I'm not always here, sent
all over the island, north, south,
you name it. No notice,

no planning. It's a job, I
suppose. If they'd told me
turf, I would have brought

a knife. This turf's wrong
too. You want stuff from the shore
hardened to salt and wind.

This'll dry up and die. Kids play
here, you can see that,
football doesn't help. We

cleared turf over there to
expose the flagstones, gets
you right down to the real

foundation, that's what
they said. It's important
they said. This is the

true floor for folk to
walk on. It's flagstones here
too, where the kids play

football – we've had it all
up and turfed it again
and again. It won't work,

parched earth and stone.
If they'd told me,
I would have brought a knife.

post-mistress

my feet endure
the seasons' floods
fingers sift, delve deeply

a ripple of postcards
on an ink-scrawled tide
stamps from Amsterdam, Lloret del Mar

where Morag had her first joint
at eighty two
reckless in the noon-day heat

and wrote to tell her son
all about it

Munlochy

The valley shines
gold from sea to hill, tree to sky
in afternoon sun, good sun, though the evening chill
promises frost, morning mist.

harbour news

whiter than white, Ullapool
binds in sunlight
tourists wading fish-reek
chips, engine oil

pebbles on the beach
skim the loch's grimy passage
harbour headlines
Spanish, French
Italian

only one day late

I was expecting Russian

Shakin Brig

dinna set fit
on the Shakin Brig
gin the Don be smooth
dinna gie a fig
for the Shakin Brig
his nae flair
fit's mair
the Shakin Brig
disnae care
fit faas
doon
doon
tae the hungert Don
gin the Don taks ane
fair the Dee taks three
we dinnae want ane
tae be you or me
sae
dinna set fit

Testament of youth

Life on a plate? Salome danced
rhythmically and well
removed each veil exquisitely
endorsing teasing symmetry

expecting more from Herod's
drunken exaltation
more than her mother said
more than a severed head

Shakespeare no more

Macbeth was never Thane of Cawdor.
Shakespeare was wrong, and yet the wood endures,
a pale cathedral, shining in the sun,
washed clean and pure.

There is no murder here, nor ever was
except the land now shattered by the gorge
burn-bruised and torn, blistered with snow-drops
pricked with holly and tourists' laughter.
The Scottish play is based on lies.
There was no murder foul, nor falsity
but battle-courage and maternal line;
Macbeth's wife had the stronger claim.
Why has she lost all public sympathy
forever banished in consumer hands
to bleak detergent fears – out, out damned spot?
She would have made a killing nowadays
floating amid the elegaic trees
beech-stained, an Ariel of the modern age,
bolder than many, branded best or worst.
Gruoch by name and nature, Boece wrote,
inventing gruesome facts to flesh the tale
ignoring southern politics; and to the end
he blames the wife, exonerates the male
the Mormaer who ruled honestly and well
with Gruoch, rightful Queen of Scotland.

Queenship has never been a sinecure.
Take Mary; impulsive, tolerant and brave
she could have won Miss World, or been Eurhythmic.
The price was wrong. She came unstuck, not down.
Misunderstood and always under-rated
(they never had the poll-tax in those days)
too beautiful, too young, she was pole-axed
wasted by Calvin and the Scottish male.
Confused, conditioned and contaminated
she tried to break the geis laid upon her
– It cam wi' a lass, and it'll pass wi' a lass
her father's words.

She died to prove they weren't meant for her.
There was no sister-feeling, intuition
Elizabeth allowed her execution
spotting an erstwhile virgin reputation
with blood that will not wash, even in Cawdor
while Mary shines as white as Cairngorm snow
fresh on the summit in the heart of spring
poised for the avalanche.

Though Scottish history is always tragic
even from tears, fresh hope will grow
wholesome and free, polyunsaturated
as Flora, who braved prison-ships and death
to help a prince who did not write to thank her.
The public did. She'd brightened up their lives
(just like a dose of Lawley did for Wogan)
adding that necessary female touch
to a sad, misdirected revolution
that ended in the death-masque of Culloden
and dies there still.
The clans were crushed, their way of life deleted
all for a few sweet songs by Rabbie Burns
and Flora, fresh with courage, emigrated
to fight a losing battle in the States
returning home to die, queen of our hearts
queen of puddings:
we cannot rise above it, yet we must.
She was not saccharine, but made from girders
no iron lady, but an iron brew
a bitter sweet that courses through the veins
a vision independent and dependable
at once good for the heart, and for the reputation
white-washed, slightly rusty at the edges.
We see her elevated by the years
above the young pretender, who dissolves
into a slurry of hard drink and mountains
till he was shipped to France and lost the mountains,
Monroes no more, nor any other clan.

And so the clans were brushed into the sea
to farm the shores and harvest kelp and sorrow
the caschrom, not the plough to till the stones
this was no land for people, only lairds.
Two women, among others, changed the highlands
fashioned a country fit for Harry Lauder
and timeshares, but for very little else:
Victoria, hiding in Balmoral heights
and Sutherland, who did not have the gaelic
to understand the suffering of her people
and thought the clearances were beneficial
leaving the land more profitable, empty
except for sheep. 'A braw bricht moonlicht nicht?'
Aye, right enough.
They did not look beyond their castle doors
but sat in towers like Ulysses' widow
spinning time, ever weaving and unpicking
they did not think, they did not see, or ask
and yet we do not censure them as harshly
as Shakespeare slated Gruoch, though the land
lies empty, ruined, fit for deer and tourists
who wonder at the 'natural' solitude
see plots of special scientific interest
not murdered land where hearts and people bled.

Shakespeare was wrong, and yet his word endures,
tossed lightly through the land, blind faith unchallenged
as slick as TV advertising slogans
as slick as any party-smart campaign
– out, out damned spot – poor Gruoch's name is mud
and where there's mud, there's brass, brass-neck, no doubt
or fire.

But set the wood alight, rethink the claims
of history as it rises in the gorge
and spills beyond the banks of truth and reason
distorts perception, carries all before it
leaving no time to seek a proper balance
between the past and present prejudices.

This is not Camelot, and not Culloden
this is not Fotheringay, this wood is Cawdor
where Gruoch did not live, nor yet Macbeth.
Spring creeps through the yearning trees
a grey-green shadow on the smaller boughs
snowdrops bloomed and died two months ago.
Now bluebells struggle through the coarser grass
and now and then a violet or primrose
shines beneath our feet, but all in vain;
our eyes fly upwards to the towering trees
we grow with them, we must, burn-bruised and torn
like Flora, Mary, Gruoch, we must rise –
and if we fall, we fall.